Becoming Bulletproof
SURVIVE & THRIVE IN ANY SITUATION

BY CARL TAYLOR

Disclaimer

All the information, techniques, skills and concepts contained within this publication are of the nature of general comment only and should not be in any way interpreted as the individual advice.

Becoming Bulletproof: Survive and Thrive in Any Situation © Carl Taylor 2020

www.carltaylor.com

First Published in Australia in 2020 by Kaizen Publishing

www.kaizenpublishing.com

All rights reserved. No part of this publication may be reproduced or transmitted by any means, electronic, photocopying or otherwise, without prior written permission of the author.

ISBN 978-0-9807632-2-5

Layout & Typesetting by Hammad - HMDgfx.com

Cover design by Mercedes Piñera

To those who supported me during my own dark times, may everyone benefit from your love through the words in this book.

Acknowledgements

No man ever stands alone. This book and the insights shared wouldn't exist without the work and support of many others.

Much of my shift in perspective over the last 10 years has come from the support and work of my coach and friend, Divya Darling, along with the incredible work of Byron Katie.

Also, without my amazing team at Automation Agency I wouldn't have been able to step away from the business long enough to go on the personal journey of discovery needed to truly embody this work in my own life and then sit down and actually write this book.

I must also acknowledge Mari, who randomly asked me what I would do differently if I knew my life would end in 12 months. Without your question, this book probably wouldn't exist.

To my amazing friends and family, I want to acknowledge you too. You are absolute inspirations to me. Our conversations helped me clarify my thoughts and message, and I'm truly grateful to have you in my life.

Finally, I would like to acknowledge you for deciding to pick up this book and read it. That in itself takes courage and a certain strength of character. It shows you value growth and learning. I am humbled and honoured to be able to share some of my journey with you.

Contents

PROLOGUE 9

1. **A TASTE OF REALITY** 13
   It's All Bullsh*t

2. **TAKE OFF THE DISGUISE** 31
   Understanding Your True Nature

3. **ARMED & DANGEROUS** 59
   How You Impact Others

4. **BULLETPROOF YOUR ARMOUR** 75
   Steps to Surviving Anything and Anyone

5. **GOING INTO BATTLE** 103
   Living a Bulletproof Life

   RECOMMENDED RESOURCES 117

   ABOUT THE AUTHOR 119

PROLOGUE

Who's *your favourite superhero?*

For me it's always been Superman.

Maybe that's because I thought my parents had just misspelled my name and I was actually Kal-El (that's Superman's real name) not Carl. More likely, it's because he represented something deeper to my core.

Superman has always been my favourite, not because he can fly or because he has x-ray vision, but because of his incredible strength, resilience and the fact that he's physically bulletproof; literally the bullets just bounce right off him.

He knows who he is and what he stands for and he doesn't compromise.

Plus, he's one of the few superheroes that was born this way. He didn't become super due to an accident, a spider bite or expensive tech, he's just being himself.

He has the power to rule the world but chooses to contribute to it instead.

It's actually frail, geeky, awkward Clark Kent that is the disguise.

I think this is what drew me most to Superman. Especially as a teenager, when I was awkward and geeky and yet I knew that was just a disguise, not the real me, where I longed to discover and show the world my Superman side.

What about you? Were you the awkward kid? The popular kid? The athletic kid? The nerdy kid?

What label did you identify with? What labels did others put on you? These labels (both internal and external) are often what we use to hide the truth of who we really are.

We hold back our own natural gifts and try to fit in with society. We desperately seek to blend in. Even those who look like they are trying to stand out are really just trying to fit in based on the disguises they're wearing.

This is something to think about as we move through this book together.

Today as I write this, I have to smile at my full-circle journey.

An entire decade has passed since I wrote my first book *Red Means Go!* where I sat in a red chair at my parents' house over Christmas 2009 and wrote the entire book in 5 days.

Now here I am, sitting in that same red chair, back at my parents' place writing *Becoming Bulletproof* the week before Christmas 2019.

My goal with this book is to open your eyes to the truth that has always been in front of you. To unlock within you the strength, courage, resilience and mental toughness of Superman. To have you tap into parts of yourself you've lost and forgotten along the way, or maybe you haven't yet discovered.

It's going to be a wild journey together. Some of it might excite you, some of it might scare you and other times you might be thinking, "What has he been smoking?" Just go with it and enjoy the ride.

I've purposely kept this book short. Far too many people buy books and don't read them. I don't want the length of the book to be a deterrent to you upgrading your thinking and your life. It's just long enough to get the message across and short enough that you can read it in a few hours and start putting it into practice.

I'm so grateful that you're here reading these words. I hope that one day we have the opportunity to meet in person and continue to share in each other's journeys.

For now, let's begin...

CHAPTER 1:
A TASTE OF REALITY
It's All Bullsh*t

"Remember, all I'm offering is the truth, nothing more."
– Morpheus (The Matrix)

Have you seen the movie The Matrix?

If you haven't, it was a sci-fi movie from the 90's starring Keanu Reeves as Neo, a character pondering the question, "What is the Matrix?"

Neo soon discovers a man named Morpheus, who offers to give him the answer but only after he chooses between two pills: a red pill or a blue pill.

According to Morpheus, "You take the blue pill, the story ends; you wake up in your bed and believe whatever you want to believe." In other words, Neo can go back to blissful ignorance and illusion.

Alternatively, "You take the red pill, you stay in Wonderland and I show you how deep the rabbit hole really goes." Meaning Neo will discover the harsh and brutal realities of what life really is.

This chapter is going to be a bit like taking the red pill. We're going to pull back the curtain together on what you perceive to be real life.

So this is your last chance. If you prefer the blue pill, close this book now and stop reading. If you prefer the red pill, then keep reading and let me show you just how much of the matrix you've been living in.

THE TRUTH

What if I told you that everything you believe to be true isn't?

It's not your fault that you believe it to be true, the majority of us do. And even for those who know it's not true, the majority of us still choose to continue to accept these "truths" to fit into society.

Let's start with a story. Maybe you've heard it before…

A young child and her mother were in the kitchen one day, cooking up a roast turkey in the oven.

The child asks her mother, "Why do you cut the sides off the turkey before putting it in the oven?"

The mother responds, "I'm not sure, it's what my mother always did, let's call her and ask."

So they call the girl's grandmother and ask her, "Why do you cut the sides off the turkey before you put it in the oven?"

The grandmother responds, "It's the way my mother used to always do it."

Luckily for them, the girl's great grandmother is still alive, so they call her up and ask her, "Why do you cut the sides off the turkey before you put it in the oven?"

Her great grandmother replies, "I had a very small oven and it was the only way I could get the Turkey to fit."

Now you may laugh at this story, but this is exactly the way the world around you works.

Everything from marriage to economics, from business to relationships, and from religions to health; there are things we do or beliefs we hold, that for the majority of us (just like the mothers cutting the ends off the turkey) we don't actually know why we do it the way we do it. We just think it's what we're supposed to do because we've not known any other way.

Let's look at a few examples of what I mean…

THE HISTORY OF MARRIAGE

Today, marriage is seen by many as a sacred act, a way of showing how deeply you love someone, a commitment. However, the history of marriage didn't come from that same place of love, it was more often a business transaction, a merging of families or a change in status on the community's social ladder.

In fact, did you know that bridesmaids were originally designed to be decoys? The bridesmaids all wore exactly the same dress as the bride and veiled their faces heavily so that if, on the way to the ceremony, a thief or rival family tried to kidnap the bride to secure the dowry (this was money that often accompanied a bride to her new husband) or to prevent the marriage from taking place, they'd grab one of the bridesmaids instead.

Yet today it's such an honour to be asked to be a bridesmaid, isn't it?

What about the simple wedding dress? Why is it that nearly everyone wears a white wedding dress? Why not other colours?

Well, in 1840, Queen Victoria wore a long white wedding dress when she married Prince Albert. The word of this spread quickly, and everyone wanted to be seen as having wealth and status like Queen Victoria, so white became the standard wedding dress colour across Western culture.

Before that time, you used to get married in your best clothes. They might have been green, red, yellow, blue — any colour, really. But now it's big business to buy the "right" wedding dress, and it must be white.

What about the diamond ring? In the late 1940's, the De Beers Consolidated Mines Ltd. company, the world's largest supplier of diamonds, ran a marketing campaign with the slogan "Diamonds Are Forever" to create the story that a diamond signifies love and commitment.

This was a carefully orchestrated strategy by the De Beers company to continue the fictional narrative that diamonds are rare and expensive (which they aren't) and keep the price of diamonds high and generate profits. They artificially controlled the supply to make it seem rare, while simultaneously generating demand by convincing young men that their love is demonstrated by how big a diamond they buy.

Fascinating, isn't it?!

You see, this is the world we live in. We walk around doing and believing things to be true without ever questioning their origin or asking why they started in the first place.

Now don't get me wrong, I'm not saying you shouldn't get married, you shouldn't have bridesmaids, or you shouldn't want to be a bridesmaid. I'm not saying you shouldn't wear a white dress or that you shouldn't get a diamond engagement ring. All I'm offering is a new perspective, a chance to open your eyes to the realisation that the way you've seen the world up until now is just a mirage. What you perceive to be irreversible truths and "the way things have always been done" originate somewhere, and that point of origin is usually a far cry from that truth's current meaning.

THE HOLIDAYS

Across most of the Western world a handful of major holidays are observed, such as Easter and Christmas, but have you ever stopped to wonder about the origin of these holidays?

I know what you're thinking, "Yes, Carl, I went to Sunday school. I know that Christmas is about the birth of Jesus and Easter is about when Jesus was crucified and then raised from the dead."

What if I told you that the only reason Easter is when it is today is because in 325 AD, Emperor Constantine wanted to bring harmony to the Roman Empire and make Christianity the official religion of the Romans.

To achieve this, he needed to bring unity to the stories that were being passed on, so he set up the first major church council, the Council of Nicaea. This council was to develop structure and consistency and create a doctrine that could be followed by the entire Roman Empire.

In the third century AD, Rome was mostly made up of Pagans, so how could the council better integrate the Christian ways into their society? By linking Christian stories to some of the existing Pagan celebrations, of course.

I'm sure you've noticed that Easter isn't on the same date every year, but have you ever wondered why? I mean Christians celebrate the birth of Jesus on the same date every year, why not his death too?

This is because the Pagan ritual Easter was designed to replace was one of fertility and new beginnings that would occur during the spring equinox.

The spring equinox, now globally referred to as the March equinox, is the day when the amount of daylight and darkness is exactly identical. For those of you in the Northern Hemisphere, this marks the end of winter and the beginning of spring, while for those of us in the Southern Hemisphere, it's the end of summer and the beginning of autumn.

So Easter's date changes every year not because of any connection to Jesus's death and resurrection but because in 325 AD the Council of Nicaea determined that Easter should fall on the Sunday following the first full moon after the spring equinox to better coincide with Pagan celebrations.

Does this surprise you? Maybe you already knew this and didn't care. Maybe it's really not important. I would actually agree that the real story of how and why Easter's date changes every year isn't that important. It's the simple fact that it is just a story, made up by a group of men more than 1600 years ago, that we continue to follow and buy into today.

What about all the chocolate eggs and bunnies we love to get during Easter? Have you ever wondered what eggs and bunnies have to do with Jesus being crucified and rising again?

Again, this has a lot more to do with the original Pagan celebrations. The bunny is a symbol of fertility, as rabbits often have multiple births, and eggs represent birth and new life.

I remember painting hard-boiled eggs and decorating them during Easter during my primary school years. Some scholars believe that the original Pagan ritual of painting eggs may have begun as a way of celebrating the laying of new eggs after a long winter without them.

And here we are, 1600+ years later, still following the same tradition, even though we have eggs available all year long.

It's easy to see how you could easily link this Pagan celebration of new life with the Christian story of Jesus's resurrection. It was a smart move that clearly paid off. I find it so fascinating though, that many Christians I speak to are blissfully unaware of the Pagan roots of their traditions.

To wrap up our deep-dive into Easter, let's look at the word "Easter." Christmas at least has the word "Christ" in it, but where did "Easter" come from?

Well scholars believe the word "Easter" comes from the Pagan goddess Eostre, the goddess of spring, fertility and new life. This makes sense, since it was the fertility and new life celebrations in the spring that were taken over by this new story.

Again, I'm not saying you can't or shouldn't celebrate and enjoy Easter or any other religious or non-religious holiday. I just want you to understand that all these traditions and practices handed down through our culture are all just made up. They all have origins, often dating back thousands of years to when life was very different, and they've simply been adapted and updated over the years.

As for Christmas, similar to Easter, many believe this is originally a Christian celebration of Jesus's birth. But was Jesus really born on December 25? Modern scholars say it's unlikely.

The Bible doesn't mention an exact birthday for Jesus, and if you follow the nativity story, it would seem he wasn't born in December at all. For example, the presence of shepherds and their sheep leads experts to believe Jesus was likely born in the spring.

So why did the Council of Nicaea, 300 years after the beginning of Christianity, settle on December 25? Well, just like with Easter, it was to coincide with existing Pagan festivals honouring Saturn, the Roman god of agriculture, and Mithra, the Persian god of light.

Why? Because, as mentioned earlier, it was far easier to convince the Pagans in Rome to accept Christianity as the empire's official religion when it fit within existing customs and activities. This allowed for a more gradual rollout with less resistance than a major sudden change.

THE RULE OF LAW

Now that we've covered holidays and marriage, it's time to examine something more concrete and modern day, like laws.

The law isn't just a story, right?

Wrong. Laws change as community values change.

There was once a time that slavery was considered a lawful and acceptable part of society, yet today this sounds barbaric and horrendous.

What's changed? The collective story that we all agree on.

That's all laws are; collectively agreed-upon stories about what we as a society believe is good behaviour and what isn't.

These beliefs have been written down and a group have collectively decided that those who don't follow the rules as written should be punished. Then we created positions in our society for people to be in charge of enforcing these rules.

I'm not saying we shouldn't have laws, or that the laws we have aren't good for society. I'm just trying to help you see that every law that you follow is something that was completely made up at some point.

If you'd like to learn more about the history of laws, I'd recommend checking out The Story of The Law by John Maxcy Zane. It's written for the layman and describes the growth and improvement of laws over time.

The key point that by now I'm hoping you're starting to get is, in the words of the late Steve Jobs, "Everything around you that you call life was made up by people that were no smarter than you."

And I mean EVERYTHING.

HUMANS, THE GREAT STORYTELLERS

In his book, Sapiens, Noah Yuval Harari explains that it was humans' ability to tell stories that allowed us to thrive and become the dominant species on the planet.

Seriously, think about this for a moment... If you took 100 chimpanzees (our closest evolutionary relative sharing 99% of the same DNA) and put them on an airplane, what would happen?

Chaos, right? They'd be screeching, swinging, fighting, moving up and down the aisle constantly, jumping over seats. Do you think they'd sit calmly waiting with their seat belts done up? Of course not.

Yet, what happens when you put 100 humans on an airplane? We sit with our seat belts done up. We respect our neighbours. Most of us try not to wake our neighbours if they are sleeping, even if we badly need to use the bathroom (or maybe that's just me).

Why do we do this?

Because we've been told and have bought into the story that when the seat belt sign is illuminated, we sit with our seat belts done up.

This is just one small example of the power of stories in enabling humans to work together in greater numbers than any other species on Earth.

This unique trait of cohesion and cooperation started with basic tribes and is now happening on a global scale — thanks in no small part to the internet and accessibility of air travel. It has enabled us to create the society we now live in.

COLLECTIVELY AGREED STORIES

You might be thinking, "Yes but these aren't stories I believe by myself; others believe them too."

And you're right. In fact, that's actually how these collectively agreed stories work.

Let's take money as an example...

An early mentor of mine once said, "Money is just an idea backed by confidence."

It took me many years to truly understand what he meant; that, like everything else, money is nothing but a story.

Think about it. Who says that piece of plastic or paper (depending on where you are in the world) in your hands is worth what it's worth? Usually the government, the banks, the shopkeepers and the public.

The monetary system wouldn't work if we didn't all agree on what everything is worth. It's a story that we've all told each other and which we all maintain together.

Without that agreement, the paper or plastic you use to buy goods and services is just a piece of material; it's not much use to most people.

I'm reminded of a quote I have on my wall at home:

"Only after the last tree has been cut down

Only after the last river has been poisoned

Only after the last fish has been caught

Only then will you find that money cannot be eaten"

Money is only valuable because we all agree it's valuable. It's as simple as that. Economists can try to complicate it further, but it all boils down to that simple fact. We've agreed upon the same story of how money works.

What about a company or corporation? I have owned several companies over the years. When we all come together towards a common goal and call ourselves a company, what are we really doing?

We are telling and buying into a collective story. This company is about this, this is what it means to be a part of this company, this group of people who sit around and do these things are a company and we call ourselves (insert name of company).

Outside of the human mind, a company doesn't exist though; it's not a tangible thing. Sure, you can buy shares in a company, but you can't physically pick a company up and hold it. You could own the building a company uses, but that isn't the actual company, that's just the place where it's located. A company is just a collective story that we've all agreed upon.

A country is yet another example. Outside of a continent that is surrounded by water calling itself a country, all other countries are just collective stories.

In Europe in particular, each country has distinct (and imaginary) borders. The source of the border lines is just a complicated group of collectively agreed-upon stories.

To further the story of what a country is, we as citizens of a country also agree upon a story of identity and what values we hold. But is it really true? Can you, for example, truly say that all people from Australia are "generous and fair"? I've met plenty of fellow Aussies that I wouldn't put in that category. And yet, Australia prides itself on this identity.

It's the same with every country. Each one has a "story" of who its people are.

Religions are exactly the same. Why do so many religions have a lot of similar principles and teachings yet perceive themselves as mutually exclusive and separate? Because their stories of what happened, who was important and how you should live your life best in service to god differs — sometimes only slightly, other times in major ways.

At the end of the day, it's just differences in the stories they tell.

That's the hidden truth that far too many of us fail to realise. It's ALL stories, all the time. EVERYTHING is a story.

It's just what we humans do; we tell stories and we collectively choose to believe the stories we are told.

I could go on and on with examples, because that is what society is, it's how the world works. It's what makes many things great in our society, while at the same time being the source of all our conflict.

4 TRUTHS FOUND DOWN THE RABBIT HOLE

- MOST PEOPLE LIVE THEIR LIVES BLINDLY
- EVERYTHING THAT EXISTS TODAY WAS ONCE MADE UP
- HUMANS THRIVE ON STORYTELLING
- IT'S ALL STORIES, ALL THE TIME. EVERYTHING IS A STORY.

CHAPTER 2:
TAKE OFF THE DISGUISE
Understanding Your True Nature

―

"There is a superhero in all of us, we just need the courage to put on the cape." – Superman

Do you know who you really are?

No, not the person you think you are, who you REALLY are!

You see, YOU are perhaps the biggest storyteller that exists, and most of the stories you make up are about YOU!

You're afraid of heights

You don't like cheese

You're shy

These are all just stories. Ultimately, the only person who told you these stories was you.

Yes, maybe others told you this in the past, or even introduced the idea, but it was you who agreed with them and reinforced that story, turning it into a belief.

Take a moment and consider:

Who you are

What you stand for

What you believe

What you don't believe (which is really another belief)

What's important to you

What's not important to you

All of these things are just stories you have told yourself.

For example, for much of my early life I identified as an "introvert" because others had labelled me shy, quiet and introverted and I believed this story. I would even tell others (as well as myself), "I'm shy. I'm introverted"

Over the last decade, however, I have decided to change my story, declaring, "I'm actually an ambivert. I get energy from people and when I'm alone." I've even said, "I'm more extroverted these days."

It's fascinating what happens when you change your story. Sometimes those around you accept it, and other times they push back because it challenges their story of who they believe you to be.

I remember saying to a friend, "I'm more extroverted these days," and they promptly responded with, "No you're not. You're definitely an introvert!" Was this friend's statement true? Or was it just THEIR story of who I am?

I heard my friend and acknowledged that this was her story of who I am and not my own, so I didn't have to take it on board.

This is the power we have. The stories we tell ourselves define us, they control the actions we take and those we don't take. They control how we interact with the world. Most importantly, they define how we feel about ourselves.

THE STORY OF YOU

There are generally two types of stories that we use to shape our sense of self:

- Identity Stories: This is Who I Am
- Incident Stories: This is What Happened to Me

IDENTITY STORIES

You may have heard of affirmations before. If you read my first book, Red Means Go!, you'll know that affirmations have great power in changing our internal dialog.

You see, we all hold certain beliefs about who we are. Things like, "I'm afraid of heights." "I don't exercise." "I'm a singer not a dancer." "I'm lazy." "I love junk food too much." "I have two left feet." "I'm not very creative." "I take things personally."

Did you notice something about these?

They all start with "I"

They are all statements

All but two start with "I am"

You're literally labelling yourself and saying this is how you are. Every time you say this to yourself, you are reinforcing this story.

When you tell a story long enough, it becomes a belief. Once it has become a belief, it controls your behaviour. Every time you behave in accordance with this belief, you build stronger connections in your brain to make this thought easier and easier to have. You are literally rewiring your brain.

If you believe you aren't good with money, you'll start to unconsciously behave in ways that reinforce this belief. Maybe you'll spend too much or lose money quickly or whatever you believe someone who is not good with money would do. Every time you do, you'll use these events as further evidence as to why you were right and reinforce the story even more. Why? Because you don't want to be wrong.

You might think, "But, Carl, I only occasionally say things like this to other people. It's more a joke than anything. I don't really mean it."

Did you know that there's always one person who hears every word you say?

Most people are so busy going through life that they aren't really listening to you, they're too worried about their own lives and the stories they're telling themselves. However the one person who hears EVERY word you say is you!

Yes, even that "just a joke" comment about yourself registers consciously or unconsciously and can provide further reinforcement to an old story or plant the seed for a new story.

I'm not saying you can't ever make fun of yourself, I'm happy to do that all the time. Just be careful with the words you use and be mindful of the stories you tell yourself about who you are. There's usually plenty of ways to laugh at yourself without creating a disempowering story.

This brings me to my next point. When it comes to your identity, stories usually come in two forms:

- Empowering Stories — these stories push you in a direction that serves your greater good, they make you feel good and happy.

- Disempowering Stories — these stories are the opposite, they hold you back and keep you stagnant, small, scared and not living your full potential.

Now, if you really want to fry your brain, consider that even your disempowering stories are actually, on some level, empowering you.

If they weren't, you wouldn't keep telling yourself that story. The fact you do is because somehow, on some level (likely subconsciously), it meets one of your human needs. Maybe it's your need for significance, or the need for certainty, or possibly connection.

For now, though, just focus on what you know consciously. Explore some of your identity stories and determine whether they are empowering or disempowering.

Take a moment to pull out a sheet of paper and finish some of these sentences.

I believe...

I am...

I don't like...

I love...

I don't believe...

I can't...

You'll quickly start to see some of the stories you've convinced yourself are true.

INCIDENT STORIES

Life is filled with incidents. First we are born, and eventually we die. While in between, we experience various events and moments that shape us.

Each moment builds upon the next. Everything has an impact: the people we meet, the conversations we have, the relationships that end in heartbreak, the things we try and give up on, the things we do well and continue, the skills we learn, the books we read and even the things people do or say to us.

The very fact that you are reading this book right now is an event that is shaping part of your story.

This is also why I'm very selective these days about what I consume, because I understand that it ALL has an impact on the stories the mind offers up about who I am.

You see, it's not the events themselves that shape who you are, it's the identity stories that are formed or reinforced based on these events.

Let me explain.

When I was 8 years old, I played soccer. All my friends played too, and it was lots of fun... until it wasn't. Some of the other kids on the team would get frustrated at my ball skills. The coach (a parent of one of the other kids) constantly berated me, calling me a girl, telling me to man up.

You know what stories I attached to these events?

I'm not good at sports

I'm not manly or masculine

I hate playing soccer

I can't kick balls

All these stories were created due to a series of events during my childhood and they followed me throughout my life, keeping me from pursuing sports, making me feel inadequate around women and leading me to avoid throwing or kicking balls.

You might wonder how a small series of events in my youth did all of that. It didn't. It just started the stories and then my mind searched for evidence throughout my life to support why these stories were true and reinforce them.

It's only been in the last 10 years that I could truly shed myself of these stories. In fact, even though I've dealt with these old stories, thoughts and beliefs stemming from these events still pop up from time to time, even though it's now 25 years after the fact.

Now I want you to understand something, and it is vitally important you get this…

The person who created these stories and shaped my identity was ME.

No one else is responsible, not the coach, not the other kids on the team.

Now you might be thinking, "But, Carl, you didn't choose for that coach to say those things to you and treat you like that. He was an adult and should've known better."

Sure, and yet his behaviour was dictated by his own stories. I can't know for sure, but it's very likely he had his own issues around masculinity to deal with. He didn't say what he said to me with the intention of creating these stories for me. That was simply what I took from the events.

Very rarely do we truly mean to harm someone by what we say and do (this will be discussed more in the next chapter).

This reminds me of a conversation I had recently with a friend of mine over dinner. We were talking about this book and I mentioned this exact concept and she said, "But when I was 6 years old, my father sat me down and told me he tried to kill himself. I didn't choose for him to do that to me."

She's absolutely right. She didn't choose for her father to say this to her; however, I explained that she did choose what this event meant to her and how it would affect her moving forward.

Not consciously, mind you. Obviously a 6-year-old doesn't have the mental development to consciously choose this, but most adults aren't consciously choosing their stories either. It's all happening beneath the surface, unconsciously.

It works like this...

An event occurs. This event might be someone saying something to you, or it may be a situation that arises around you, or it could even be a thought in your own mind.

This event triggers a reaction from your mind.

Your subconscious mind reacts and attaches a meaning to this event.

This meaning might be in the form of a story like "I'm worthless", "They don't love me", "I need to help them" etc..

The meaning you attach to the event will be unique to you.

It doesn't even have to be a logical thought. It can be an emotional reaction like Sadness, Anger, Anxiety, Fear etc.. as they are just a neural pathway that gets triggered and creates a sensation.

Once the mind has attached this meaning to the trigger event, it holds on to this and if another event in the future manages to trigger this same neural pathway you can keep reliving this same story you created over and over, throughout your life.

This story posted anonymously on a forum is a great example:

> *One year, when I was a child, my father got drunk and violent at Christmas. I had just unwrapped a present, a bottle of hand lotion, when he exploded in an alcoholic rage. Our Christmas was disrupted. It was terrible. It was frightening for the whole family. Now, thirty-five years later, when I smell hand lotion*

I immediately feel all the feelings I did that Christmas: the fear, the disappointment, the heartache, the helplessness, and an instinctive desire to control.

As I said to my friend, "Your father didn't come to you and tell you this to impact you for life and give you the story you've taken from it. It was you who created that meaning inside of yourself."

Now let's make one thing clear: not all stories and meanings you make are bad.

I'm not saying you need to stop making meanings out of events in your life. Frankly, I don't know if that's even possible. We humans are meaning-making machines.

It's about realising that our stories either empower us or disempower us. And if you're going to be making meaning out of something anyway, why not choose to make an empowering story over a disempowering one?

This reminds me of another story my friend Pete told me a few years ago about these two brothers whose father was in prison for drugs and the murder of his wife. Ten years later, they were asked about it by a journalist.

One of the brothers had been in and out of jail himself over the years, mixed up in gangs, drugs and petty theft. When asked how his life ended up this way he said, "With a father like mine, how could I have turned out any differently?"

The other brother, who had become a social worker supporting those suffering from drug addiction and had a wife and kids was living (by many people's standards) a great life.

The journalist asked him the same question about how his life ended up this way, his response was, "With a father like mine, how could I have turned out any differently?"

The event these brothers experienced was exactly the same, but the stories they made about the event and what those stories meant for them were completely different.

Our stories massively shape our identity. In fact, they ARE our identity.

In chapter 4, we'll explore how you can actively choose better stories and even undo old stories that are no longer serving you.

Is It Good or Is It Bad? We'll See…

I'd like to share with you one of my favourite Chinese proverbs. It's about a farmer who is working his fields every day and one day wakes up to find that one of his horses has escaped and run away.

His neighbours say to him, "What bad luck."

The farmer responds, "We'll see."

The next day, the farmer goes out to the paddock to find that the horse has returned and brought with it two wild horses.

His neighbours say, "You now have three horses. How lucky you are!"

The farmer simply replies, "We'll see."

The following day, the farmer's son is out riding the wild horses, trying to tame them, and he falls and breaks his leg.

The neighbours say, once again, "Oh, that's a bad omen. Clearly these horses are nothing but trouble."

The farmer simply says, "We'll see."

The following day, the military comes through the village to recruit young men for the war. Because the son has a broken leg, they let him stay home.

The neighbours once more say, "What incredible luck it was that he broke his leg!" To which the farmer once again replies, "We'll see."

What I like most about this story is how well it demonstrates our limited vision on what a situation means or doesn't mean.

When we label a situation as terrible, we are looking at it from a very small and limited perspective. We are only looking at it in a very short-term perspective, we can't see the next two or three decades in front of us where this situation may be absolutely pivotal.

Every situation is neutral. It's neither good, nor bad. It just is.

It's only in our minds that we apply labels to a situation such as "bad luck" or "good luck."

I remember attending a seminar around 8 years ago where the presenter said, "Everything is nothing except the meaning you give it." It's taken 8 years for me to truly understand the wisdom in this statement.

THE HALLUCINATIONS OF THE MIND

The mind is a trickster, it's constantly coming up with hallucinations that don't exist.

What do I mean by hallucinations?

Well, let's consider for a moment that, as we've already been discussing, the world around us (and our own internal world) is made up of stories.

Consider the concept of time. Humans move through time in a linear fashion. We start at one point and move forward to another point; however, physicists believe that time-space is actually non-linear. (I won't bore you with a physics lesson here, but I encourage you to look this up if the idea interests you.)

So let's accept the fact that for us as humans, time only ever exists in this exact moment. The past doesn't exist anymore, as it's already occurred. The future doesn't exist, because it hasn't happened yet. Only this exact moment exists for us.

When you think of memories of the past, does that moment still exist? When you think about possibilities of the future, does that moment exist yet?

No, they are both hallucinations. Simply stories you're telling about these non-existent events.

In fact, evidence shows that our recollections of the past are inherently flawed. If a group of us got together and described an event we all attended, our memories would not completely line up. This is why police seek multiple eyewitness accounts to determine the truth of an event.

Everything your mind offers you is really a hallucination.

If you are stuck worrying or obsessing over a past event, you are in a hallucination. It doesn't exist because that moment is over for you, and your memory of the moment is not an accurate representation of what happened anyway.

If you are anxious about a future event that may occur, you are in a hallucination. This moment also doesn't exist, although there is an argument that it exists in what is known as "the field of potentiality" as one of infinite potential futures that could play out from this moment, but for the sake of brevity you'll have to read up on the multiverse and decision splitting to learn more about this concept.

In my experience, most of these hallucinatory futures I imagine in my mind never manifest. Would it be fair to say the same is true for you?

And what about those past hallucinations where we imagine what could have happened, had we done things differently, said one thing instead of another or acted one way and didn't act a different way.

This is all complete fantasy hallucination. If you catch yourself in that loop, just tell your mind to stop.

You said what you said, you did what you did. It was exactly what you were supposed to say and do.

How do I know? Because that's exactly what you did say and do to get to this exact moment you're in now. It's now actually a fact, it's an event that has happened. Any further thoughts about you doing anything differently is just a hallucination.

HANDLING HALLUCINATIONS

So if it's all just hallucinations, what can we do?

Notice them come up, because they will.

Once you realise you're in a hallucination, stop and thank the mind for the hallucination and remind yourself that that's exactly what it is. You don't need to stress over it, you don't need to get anxious. Just come back to the moment you're in and make a decision based on what makes the most sense in that moment. When you're in another moment later, you can make another decision if you need to.

The freedom you can find in this is incredible. This concept alone has provided the biggest freedom and sense of peace I've ever experienced.

The realisation that the only thing that exists is this moment and everything else is a hallucination removed a huge amount of anxiety from my life. For much of my adult life, I'd walked around with a level of anxiety just sitting there in the background. I didn't realise it at the time, only now when it's gone do I notice the lack of it.

This anxiety came from living in my head. I've always been a highly strategic thinker, trying to stay six moves ahead. This gave me a lot of power in business and strategy games like chess, but it also gave me a lot of anxiety, stress and unnecessary suffering. I was constantly seeing potential futures (most of them bad), yet none of them actually existed.

You may be thinking, "Surely there is value in thinking ahead," and I agree with you. It's all about context and having the choice of when you use the mind and when you say "no."

You've got to learn to be the master of your mind, not just let your mind control you.

THE REAL YOU

So who are you, really? Is it just whatever story you decide to tell yourself or is there something more to it? I guess this depends on whether you believe there's more to you than flesh, bones and chemical reactions happening inside your body.

Maybe you believe there is a consciousness to the universe and that part of that consciousness lies within you as what is commonly referred to as a "spirit" or "soul."

I'm not going to try to tell you what's true or not, because it's not my place to give you that story. It's also not necessarily my place to tell you what I believe, for what I believe right now may change in the future. What I can tell you is a question I've enjoyed pondering at various times in my life: "Am I a spiritual being having a human experience or am I a human being having a spiritual experience?"

Throughout my life, there have been various experiences that have given me pause and a deeper sense of connection to something greater than the individual known as "Carl."

What I know is that scientifically speaking, based on our current understanding of the universe, we have evidence to support this idea of a connection to something greater than ourselves.

The entire universe is made up of particles and waves that vibrate at various frequencies. These particles make up the atoms that make up the molecules that form the various chemicals and compounds within the universe. These chemicals and compounds are inside me, they are inside you and they are also spread throughout the universe; they make up all living and non-living things.

As the popular astrophysicist Neil deGrasse Tyson so eloquently said... "We are not figuratively, but literally stardust."

In a 2008 Time interview, Tyson was asked to share the most astounding fact he knew about the universe:

> The most astounding fact is the knowledge that the atoms that comprise life on Earth, the atoms that make up the human body, are traceable to the crucibles that cooked light elements into heavy elements in their core under extreme temperatures and pressures.
>
> These stars, the high mass ones among them, went unstable in their later years. They collapsed and then exploded scattering their enriched guts across the galaxy. Guts made of carbon, nitrogen, oxygen and all the fundamental ingredients of life itself.
>
> These ingredients become part of gas cloud that condense, collapse, form the next generation of solar systems stars with orbiting planets, and those planets now have the ingredients for life itself.
>
> So that when I look up at the night sky and I know that yes, we are part of this universe, we are in this universe, but perhaps more important than both of those facts is that the Universe is in us.

When I reflect on that fact, I look up – many people feel small because they're small and the Universe is big – but I feel big, because my atoms came from those stars.

There's a level of connectivity.

That's really what you want in life, you want to feel connected, you want to feel relevant you want to feel like a participant in the goings on of activities and events around you.

That's precisely what we are, just by being alive...

When you add this knowledge to the understanding that in physics and chemistry there is a law known as the "conservation of energy" (that energy can neither be created nor destroyed, it can only be transformed or transferred from one form or another), you can start to appreciate that nothing ever truly dies.

So if nothing truly dies, it stands to reason that we never truly die. We simply transform.

Even if we are just flesh and bones and nothing more, when our bodies decompose they don't just disappear, they break down and turn back into the basic elements of life, becoming fuel for other living organisms while we continue to live on as part of the universe.

Understanding this, without any spiritual or religious connotations, it's hard to not feel like there is a greater connectedness to the universe than may first appear on the surface.

The real you, the true you, is far greater than the labels and stories you put on yourself.

You are part of the universe. You are part of the interconnectedness that is all of us. Simply by existing you are these things. You don't need to do anything for this to be true.

NO ONE CAN EVER TRULY KNOW YOU

For many of us, all we really desire is to feel known and that others truly see us.

This is a beautiful sentiment, and there are many ways for people to deeply connect while pulling back layers of stories to better see the other's true self (eye gazing, which is discussed in chapter four, is one such activity). However, I don't believe anyone will ever truly know the YOU that you know.

What do I mean by this?

Even your closest family members, romantic partners and friends you've known forever — none of them will ever truly know who you are. They'll only know the story they've created about who you are.

Just as you have a story about yourself, they have a story about you. This story can be updated, of course, yet it's still only a story, it can never be a true representation of ALL that you are.

Let me give you a simple and practical example. I'm allergic to peanuts. I've told my friends and family this countless times, yet even my own mother will sometimes forget. Sometimes when I tell a friend (who I previously told) that I am allergic to peanuts, they act like they are hearing this information for the first time.

Does this mean they don't listen to me or don't care? No, of course not. It just means that this fact wasn't a strong element in the story they hold of who I am, particularly compared to the importance that I attribute to this story of who I am.

Even if you could somehow share all your deepest and most intimate stories of who you are with another person what they would hear and what they would retain as part of their story of who you are would not be the same. We are always experiencing life via our own stories of who we are and what certain things mean.

The same is true in reverse. This means you will never truly know your friends, family, partners or children the way they know themselves. Your stories may overlap, but they won't match.

This is also something that happens during dating. Have you ever noticed that when you first start dating someone, you feel like nothing they do is ever wrong, like they're perfect?

And yet, often the very trait or behaviour you found endearing at the start of the relationship can be one of the main causes of friction years later.

What changed?

Well, apart from the oxytocin high that typically wears off around the 2-year mark of a relationship, the other thing that changed is your story of who your partner is and what that behaviour or trait means.

The good news is you can recreate the oxytocin levels simply by changing your story again.

If you have a significant other, try this activity:

For the next two weeks, focus solely on the things you admire and like about them. Really appreciate the good; don't get caught up in the friction. I know that might seem hard, but it's only for two weeks.

I bet your level of love and attraction for your partner increases. This is how simply we can change our stories, by changing what we focus on.

This activity isn't only true for your romantic partners, you can try a similar activity for yourself.

For the next two weeks (I actually recommend forever, but let's start with two weeks), focus on what you appreciate about yourself. Think about what you like about you and tell yourself you love you.

Look in a mirror, make eye contact with yourself and say, "I love you."

Why do this? Because this is who you really are. You are an incredible human being that is loved and connected to the entire universe simply by being alive.

The rest of it is all just a story.

4 REMINDERS FOR YOUR TRUE SELF

- BE MINDFUL OF YOUR IDENTITY & INCIDENT STORIES

- YOU'RE GOING TO MAKE UP A STORY ANYWAY, YOU MAY AS WELL MAKE IT AN EMPOWERING ONE!

- WE ARE ALL CONNECTED. YOU ARE LITERALLY STARDUST

- YOU ARE THE ONLY PERSON WHO WILL TRULY KNOW YOU

CHAPTER 3:
ARMED & DANGEROUS
How You Impact Others

"With great power, comes great responsibility."
– Uncle Ben (Spiderman)

Imagine if everyone in the world walked around with a loaded gun. At any moment, someone could shoot you or someone you cared about. Well the truth is that we all have a loaded weapon: our body. The bullets in our weapon are our words and actions.

Every word you say has the power to be a wounding bullet. Every action you take has the power to destroy just as much as it does to create.

I think that far too many of us have forgotten just how powerful we are in influencing other people's lives. In fact, in every moment you are either manipulating or being manipulated. You may not be conscious of it, you may not mean to do it, but you're doing it.

Let me ask you this... Have you ever done something for someone with complete love, respect and good intentions, yet they've taken it the wrong way and been hurt, upset or angry by what you did?

Why did this happen? Simply because their story around the action was different than your story.

They may have had prior incident stories, identity stories about themselves, identity stories about you or, more than likely, some combination of all these types of stories. It was this unique combination that led to their interpretation of the event being different than yours.

This brings me to a very important point: For a word or action to become an injuring bullet, only one person in a given interaction needs to see it as such.

We are constantly firing bullets, and it is the recipient of the bullet, not the person firing the bullet, who decides if the bullet causes damage or not.

It's easy to see when you bring a group of people together, how easy it can be to create massive damage. Through the entire interaction, you are all firing bullets at each other, constantly creating the potential for a bullet to pierce the skin and sink in as a new story or to reinforce an old story.

Just as my childhood soccer coach couldn't control how I interpreted his words and actions, you too cannot control how what you say or what you do will be received. I'd even go as far as to say it's not your responsibility how others receive what you say and do. How the other person receives something is on them, no matter your intentions.

What is your responsibility, though, is to be mindful of the energy and intention behind the words and actions that come from you.

If you are acting from a space of love or genuine care, then you can know that your intentions were genuine, and the rest is up to them.

So now you might be thinking, "Hooray! I don't have to care if I hurt someone's feelings or do something that upsets someone else."

And to that I would say yes, it's not your responsibility as long as you had no intention to cause them harm. I'd also say that to simply not care that you unintentionally caused harm would be a bit too callous if it were me.

If I hurt someone I care about, then of course I'm going to care. I'm going to want to communicate and clear up the misunderstanding as best I can. Yet this can sometimes lead to even more misunderstandings, or sometimes others will not accept my attempts to address confusion due to their own heightened emotions. When this happens, that's when I tell myself that I've done what I can; if they want to remain hurt, that's on them.

Remember, however, the same is also true for you. If you feel hurt, upset or angry by what someone else has done or said, that responsibility lies purely with you. You let the bullet in, you saw it as a bullet and you caused the damage.

It doesn't matter if their intention was loving or their intention was to cause harm. The person who decided it was a bullet that would create damage and not just bounce right off you was you.

Let me give you a few examples.

I am going on a trip to Israel soon and I invited my mother to join me. She declined because she believed the time of year I was planning on going would be too hot.

I spoke to my friend who is organising the trip and shared my mother's concerns, and she said, "It will only be hot in Egypt, but the rest of the trip will be very comfortable."

I relayed this message back to my mother... "Just letting you know, I spoke to my friend and she says it won't be 40 degrees anywhere except Egypt, so you can think about that."

A bit later during a discussion with my mother I learned that she had taken my comment to mean, "You're wrong," when instead my intention was to say, "If you want to reconsider and come, I'd love to have you."

Now you might wonder why didn't I just say that. That's a great question. Why is it that we humans don't just come out and say exactly what we mean? Why do we speak in cryptic messages so often? I don't have an answer for you. All I know is that communicating more clearly in situations like this to avoid misfires is an area I need to work on.

Hopefully you always speak in clear language to convey exactly what you mean to say. Unfortunately for me, it's still a work in progress.

The other important point to note here is that at no point did I say to my mother, "You're wrong," yet that's exactly how she interpreted my message.

You see, it was her mind leveraging her own identity and incident stories to spin the message that suited her own internal narrative of what happened.

She does it, I do it and you do it too!

If we accept that it's going to happen, then what can we do when someone says something that we find hurtful?

There are two things I recommend:

- If you are still in the situation, you can ask them to clarify what they mean. A simple "What exactly are you saying?" would suffice.

- If you are no longer in the situation, you can use the process that I'll be sharing in the next chapter to examine your thoughts and consider the meaning you've taken from the words or actions of this person and reflect on other possible truths.

A woman I met recently shared a perfect story about clarifying the meaning of a statement.

Her grandmother often said the phrase "That hides a multitude of sins" when observing what a family member was wearing. This woman, her mother and her sister would always be horrified that her grandmother would say such a thing, their interpretation was that it was not a nice thing to say.

One day this woman decided to actually clarify with her grandmother what she meant, and asked, "Grandma, what exactly are you trying to say?"

"I'm just saying that you look really nice," her grandmother responded.

Instantly it became clear that the wounds were being created by the family members' interpretations, not the grandmother's meaning. Why? Because they each had different stories about what that saying meant.

TRUTHS, FACTS AND RESPECT

You may be thinking, "Well, if everything we believe is just a story, then all truths are subjective." I would agree with that statement but would also point out that there is a difference between truth and fact.

Let me explain.

In the world today there has been a strong rise in younger generations accepting that people can have their individual "truths." The saying "You do you" comes to mind.

I fully subscribe to this concept. I have a favourite line in the Broadway musical Jesus Christ Superstar where Pontius Pilate says, "We both have truths — are yours the same as mine?"

I was actually pondering this line in my early 20's when I first started to see that each of us hold subjective truths, individual stories we have bought into that may not align.

Understanding this gave me a new respect for others and their perspectives. If I had lived the same life they had, experienced all the same events and created the same stories, then I would believe the same things. I would think just like them and act in the exact same way; therefore, I had no right to judge others for who they are or what they say or do.

Sadly, it seems most people don't take this approach. Even those who are into personal truths seem to only accept the truths of others until they clash with their own truths.

Now I also come from a highly scientific background. My mother was a high school science teacher, my uncle has a PhD in mathematical biology, my father worked in electronics, my sister is in health science, and I wanted to be an inventor as a child, so let's just say I grew up learning to question everything and constantly look for evidence.

Any true scientist will tell you that they only follow the evidence. They don't hold on to their scientific principles as absolute fact. They believe them to be the best-known truth based on the current evidence.

A true scientist will welcome new data and be excited to have their theories and experiments proved wrong. It is thrilling for a scientist to be proven wrong, because this translates into new discoveries and new knowledge, which is what science is all about. Unfortunately, human ego can get in the way of this — even within the scientific community.

I'm often frustrated when I see people on various sides of debates who are so resolute in their "rightness" that they won't even entertain someone else's point of view to see what could be learned. This arrogance often stands in the way of true discovery.

As I mentioned, since I can see why someone might believe the things they believe and think the things they think, I can't judge them. Likewise, I try to take the fence sitter approach in any argument, encouraging people to present me with both points of view and forming my own opinion while still being open to having my mind changed again later.

For example, I was once at a party where I met a guy who was adamant that the moon landings were faked. Although I disagreed with him, I listened to his argument.

Later, after I came home, I looked up and watched a documentary about why it's obvious the moon landing was faked. I came away from that documentary thinking, "That makes a lot of sense. It probably really was faked."

A week later, I decided I needed more data, so I watched a documentary about why people who believe the moon landing was faked are wrong. I came away from that saying, "Clearly this actually happened, and the fake arguments are wrong."

Now which is true? I don't know, because I haven't personally done my own testing or experiments to verify. I've heard arguments on both sides and I'm a realist enough to know that there's probably a bit of truth in both arguments.

I have my opinions based on the evidence presented, but I cannot say with absolute certainty that my opinion is the fact of how it happened because I don't have all the data. I wasn't there.

So I can put my faith in the people who have collected the data and choose to accept certain truths to be current known facts. That doesn't mean future evidence couldn't change my thinking, as any good scientist will tell you, it's just my best understanding based on the science as it stands today.

So what's a fact and what's a truth?

Truths are beliefs, like religion, god, stories of self or stories of others. A fact is something that can be measured. Facts go beyond theories or beliefs. They're proven through calculation and experience and can be tested by others. I would also call an event that occurred in the past a fact.

Even still, facts are not immovable. New data and research can be uncovered that changes the measurements and therefore the facts.

Facts are just a different kind of truth. A mutually confirmed truth based on the evidence presented.

Fact: I can't fly without the help of some type of technology — a hot air balloon, an airplane, a helicopter, a wing suit, a wind tunnel, etc. No matter what story I tell myself, this has been proven to be a fact over and over. Yet I have heard stories of Yogis who supposedly can levitate off the ground with nothing but the power of their mind. As I have not seen any measured evidence of this claim, however, I cannot say it is fact.

The existence of a god or gods is a truth. As far as I know, we haven't been able to test for or prove the existence of such a being or universal intelligence. Until that can be done, the existence of what many would label as "god" cannot be a fact, but that doesn't mean it's not true for those who choose to believe.

THE WAR OF TRUTHS

The scientist in me gets concerned about the lack of objectivity that can accompany the current personal truths movement. The "you do you" movement.

For example, if you believe the Earth is flat, I can respect that the life you've lived has led you to the point where you now believe this; however, when you can do your own experiments to try to prove the earth is flat and have the results actually demonstrate that there is in fact a curvature to the earth and you still continue to believe it's flat (as can be seen in the documentary *Behind the Curve*), then in this situation you are just stuck in a story of denial. You are not accepting the evidence, nor are you presenting your own strong evidence to counter the evidence we currently use to call it a fact.

This blindness to updating a truth isn't just on the flat earthers; scientists and scholars can be just as bad.

There is one particularly notable public figure atheist (who I won't mention by name) who often lashes out at religious people with the same prejudice and certainty in the argument that god doesn't exist and that those who believe in god are idiots. This person exhibits the same closed-minded attitude that they often call out in some people of faith. Choosing to solely focus on areas of disagreement, never willing to consider grounds of commonality.

If the story of a god or universal intelligence brings peace and happiness to your life, then it's a story that's serving you. As long as that belief is causing no harm to others who don't believe, then I don't see a problem.

Likewise, if the belief that there is no god and that we as humans and the universe is one big random fluke and that every event is random with no meaning whatsoever brings peace and happiness to your life, then that's clearly serving you too, so feel free to believe it.

When we all start to understand that there are truths and facts, and that even facts are just other forms of truths, we can all start to be far more understanding of others' perspectives while also being able to educate and challenge (as well as be challenged by) other points of view.

Just be mindful if you are challenging someone else's personal truths; this is their identity story you are ultimately challenging, so do it with the intention to empower them, not to disempower them or serve your own ego of feeling right. If you truly care for them, you wouldn't want to challenge a thought or story that empowers them simply because you don't agree with it.

Remember, it's our words and actions that impact those around us. We hold the power to create and destroy in our bodies every moment of every day. Use it wisely.

4 INSIGHTS AS YOU ENGAGE WITH OTHERS

- EVERY WORD YOU SPEAK IS A FIRING BULLET
- ONLY THE RECIPIENT CONTROLS IF THE BULLET WOUNDS
- SEEK CLARITY IN THE INTENT BEFORE CREATING MEANING
- TRUTHS ARE PERSONAL, FACTS ARE OBSERVABLE

CHAPTER 4:

BULLETPROOF YOUR ARMOUR

Steps to Surviving Anything and Anyone

"Everything happens at exactly the right moment, neither too soon nor too late. You don't have to like it... It's just easier if you do."
– Byron Katie

Note: If you've skipped straight to this chapter to get to the "good stuff," I encourage you to read the previous chapters first. As the saying goes, context is key. To get the most out of the strategies shared in this chapter, having context helps.

Back in chapter one, I introduced the story of *The Matrix* and the character Neo.

SPOILER ALERT: One of my favourite scenes in this movie is towards the end when Neo is fighting two agents (these are the bad guys) in a hallway. The agents draw their guns and fire at Neo, completely emptying their clips.

Neo just stands there calmly, raises his hand out in front of him and says, "No." The bullets slow and finally stop in mid-air, a few inches in front of him. Neo looks at the bullets and they fall to the ground.

In this chapter, I aim to give you this same ability.

I want you to have the ability to calmly watch bullets being fired at you and simply say "no" and watch as the bullets stop in their tracks.

Does that sound good?

Not only do I want you to have the ability to stop bullets before they hit you, I also want you to have Superman's strength so that even if a bullet does hit you, it can just bounce right off.

Are you ready?

THERE ARE NO MISTAKES

What if I told you that everything that has happened in your life was for a reason? That every single event, conversation and person you came into contact with was serving you and your future. That there are no mistakes in your life, there is nothing you need to regret.

You may choose, as some do, to believe this is due to a divine destiny or fate, or you may simply tell yourself this as a better and more empowering story that envisions there are lessons in everything and you can use these to move towards a better future.

Whatever best helps you accept this story as true is up to you. All I can tell you is that this is a story worth buying into.

Life became far easier and happier once I started to tell myself this story and truly buy into the idea that life happens *for* me, not to me. That every moment in my life has happened exactly as it should. Nothing has been too early or too late.

Now, I accept that many in the scientific community may scoff at this idea, saying life is random and there is no meaning in it, we are simply a cosmic fluke from millennia of failures in the evolution of the universe. And I wouldn't argue. I accept that this could indeed be just as true.

All I know is that in my own experience when I tell myself the story that it's all random and meaningless, it doesn't fill me with the same sense of peace and happiness I have when I believe the former.

So if it is, as it now should very well be clear that it is, my choice what stories I tell myself about the world, and I can choose between these two stories, why wouldn't I choose the one that makes my life and the lives of those around me better?

WHY WE SUFFER

What is suffering?

It's telling ourselves that a situation that is currently a certain way, shouldn't be that way. That it should be something different.

What if you stopped telling yourself that a situation should be different? What if you realised that right now you are exactly where you are meant to be? That everything in your past has been leading up to this exact moment, and that this moment is just another point in the journey to your better future.

It can be hard to swallow, I get it. But if life is just the stories we tell ourselves, why tell yourself a story that makes you suffer?

Have you ever looked back on your life and connected the dots? That if this specific event hadn't happened exactly as it did, you wouldn't have then done that amazing thing 5 years later.

I certainly have. Many of the things that at the time seemed terrible turned out to be the very things that helped shape my life into the incredible life I now enjoy.

For example, I was bullied during my school years, however it was this bullying that led me to develop the story that I would get back at my tormentors by "owning them one day." This story led me into the world of business, wealth creation and, ultimately, personal development. So much of my life is the way it is today because I was bullied.

At the time it was terrible and I suffered, however decades on, I now look back on that experience with gratitude. I can see the benefits in how it shaped me and the incredible life I get to live today.

The tricky part is we can only connect these dots when we look backward into our pasts. Our vision is too limited to be able to connect the dots looking forward into the future. Many of us try, but we're only in hallucination. We have no crystal ball, we can only control the meanings we make in this moment right now.

So instead of trying to fight whatever situation you are currently facing, why not trust that you are exactly where you need to be, and that this is a dot that will connect with clarity and obviousness to another dot at some point down the line, just as it has for you in the past.

Trust that life has your back. That you have your back. That this moment contains a lesson. Once you can find the lesson and truly learn it, it's only going to get better from here.

TO COMPARE IS TO DESPAIR

Since suffering comes from not accepting life as it is and instead wishing it were different, what is the major source of this type of thinking?

Comparison!

In any situation where you compare yourself to someone else, you are immediately opening yourself up to thinking consciously or unconsciously that your current situation is not as you'd like it to be.

There are countless ways to compare:

Comparing yourself to others

Comparing your partner to others

Comparing your house to another house

Comparing your body

Comparing your wealth

Comparing your business

Comparing your abilities

As Mark Twain so perfectly stated, "Comparison is the death of joy." There will always be someone faster, smarter and more experienced than you. Making a habit of comparing yourself to others will result in perpetual disappointment.

Now I'm not saying you have to just accept your situation and not do anything to change it if you so desire. All I'm saying is any suffering and anguish you have because of this thought is 100% in your control and your choice.

You can choose to suffer and be miserable or you can choose to accept what is and be happy.

You see once you are happy with what is, that doesn't mean you can't still make decisions to move toward a new and different future, it just means you don't fight reality and suffer.

The next time you find yourself comparing or feeling that a situation isn't how you want it to be, use the technique I'm about to share with you to examine your thoughts from different perspectives.

RELEASING YOUR STORIES

So how can you change your story?

First, you don't always have to know what your story is to change it. Our habits are neural pathways that fire regularly, so they are the paths of least resistance. If you want to stop a neural pathway from being triggered, skip the trigger or work to rewire or re-associate it with something else.

Have you ever had a song instantly remind you of a moment or person in your life? This is a trigger that starts a neural pathway connection.

If you feel a negative emotion surfacing, you are being triggered. Don't worry about the story that created it, just take a deep breath (5 seconds in through the nose) and let out a deep audible sigh through the mouth. As you let out that sigh, imagine your heart opening, almost like a flower blooming from your chest. Feel the emotion like a blast of energy being released from your chest.

This might sound a bit silly and weird, but I encourage you to try it and see the release and peace this can bring you.

In fact, using our imagination (like visualising a flower and energy blooming from your chest) is a powerful tool in managing our emotions.

EXAMINE YOUR STORIES

The simple breathe-and-release technique is an easy way to let go of emotions that are surfacing and affecting you without having to do the work to examine the source of these emotions. However, sometimes it can help to go deeper and release a story completely.

Maybe it's a story that keeps looping and coming up over and over, or maybe you've found that breathe-and-release didn't cut it for you. In these cases, I recommend that you spend time examining your thoughts and beliefs to understand the underlying stories or truths that are fueling your reactions and work to address them.

Byron Katie, author of Loving What Is, teaches an incredible process I highly recommend and personally use regularly. She calls it "The Work" and it's one of the most profound and yet simple techniques I've learned in my years of studying human psychology.

The process is essentially to ask yourself four questions and then examine your thoughts from other possible points of view and consider the truth in these other perspectives.

To illustrate this, I'd like to use an example from my own past. In a previous relationship, I created a lot of friction because of my story that I wanted to travel the world, living and working from anywhere.

My thought was, "My partner should want to travel with me."

According to Katie, the first question you ask yourself is: Is it true? Is it true that my partner should want to travel with me? "Yes," I would respond.

That brings us to the second question: Can I absolutely know that it's true?

This question is a great one. I very rarely can answer this question with anything but a "no." It's certainly possible to decide that you can absolutely know that something's true, so it's ok if your answer to this is affirmative.

In this situation, I would often realise, "No, I can't absolutely know that it's true that my partner should want to travel with me. How could I know that? I'm not her, and I don't know what my life's future will hold."

Now that we've established the truth (or not) of this thought, the next step is to see how it impacts us.

Ask yourself: How do I react when I have this thought?

This essentially prompts you to examine the thoughts and behaviours that this thought (aka story) is creating in you.

For this example, I might say, "I get annoyed with her. I hold myself back from traveling. I feel sad and trapped. I think I'm in the wrong relationship. I snap at her. I impose my own values on her."

Take your time here to truly examine how you are reacting in the situation, within yourself and with the other people involved, all because of your belief in this thought.

Once you are clear on how you've been reacting, now comes the really powerful part. Ask yourself the final question: Who would I be without this thought?

I find this to be the most powerful question of them all. Instantly, it starts to shift how I feel about a given situation.

In this example, I might say, "I'd be loving and accepting and appreciate her for who she is. I'd organise my own travel and tell her I'd love for her to join me but if she chooses not to come, I'll still love her and I'll be back with lots of photos and stories to share."

Can you feel the difference in the energy, emotion and intention when I articulate who I would be without this thought that's creating friction?

By this stage in the process I'm typically already feeling different about the situation, and yet there's one more step that can take it even further. It's one of the more interesting (and sometimes challenging) parts of the process, what Katie calls "The Turnaround."

This is where you take your original thought and turn it around. Take who your thought is about and swap it to yourself. Then you take your story and reverse it.

For example, the thought, "My partner should want to travel with me," becomes, "I should want to travel with me," when I swap it to myself.

Then you consider what truths have been revealed through this new perspective.

In this example, I thought about how I should want and be okay with travelling by myself. That maybe there's some fear in me about traveling solo, which is why I really wanted her to come with me. Maybe it was my own anxiety driving this thought, rather than a true need for her to come with me.

Another turnaround in the reversal approach could be using the reverse language. In this example, I would switch "should" with "shouldn't," making the statement: "My partner shouldn't want to travel with me."

Again, let's consider what truths are in this statement. Why should my desire to travel be imposed on another person? Maybe I'm actually a pain to travel with and it's better for our relationship if we don't travel together.

This is just an example, of course. My ex and I actually did travel a lot and got on fine while doing it. Yet this is a real example from my life of a thought that created friction and the ways in which I considered other possible truths to better understand myself and my stories.

The power of examining a thought from other points of view and finding the truths in these alternate perspectives can often release deep attachments you may have had to your original thought.

When you release the charge of emotion that surrounds a thought, you can act from a more centred space to gain clarity, move forward or even just dismiss the thought altogether as if it never existed.

Pain vs Suffering

Since almost everything in this world is a story then it makes sense that the source of ALL our suffering comes from the stories we tell ourselves.

But first let me clarify that there is a difference between pain and suffering.

If you are in an accident and lose your leg, you will likely experience physical pain, possibly even some phantom pain. I'm not saying that if you tell yourself the story "I'm not in pain" that the pain will magically go away. That's just fighting reality and not accepting that in this moment you are supposed to be feeling pain.

The distinction between pain and suffering is that pain is a physical response from signals your body is sending you about an event. Suffering comes from your interpretation of the meaning of this event.

Therefore, suffering because of your lost leg is a choice.

You could tell yourself the story that your life is over, that you'll never be loved again, that you're not the person you once were, that you're disabled — or whatever disempowering story you wish to tell yourself — and suffer now and into the future.

Alternatively, you can tell yourself that losing your leg gives you a new perspective of appreciation for all your other working limbs, that it gives you the opportunity to explore new technologies and uncover new parts of your identity, that your leg clearly wasn't necessary for your life moving forward because otherwise you'd still have it.

I know how that last one sounds. Bear with me here.

Consider that if you lose your leg yet you're still alive, doesn't that suggest that you don't need your leg to live your life?

I would argue that the sheer fact you no longer have that leg and are not dead is evidence that this leg wasn't necessary for your life moving forward. That whatever your future holds, it doesn't require this leg. If it was needed, you'd still have it.

Any beliefs or suffering you have around needing this leg would be due to the stories you're holding onto about a future that you'd hallucinated where this leg still existed.

Maybe it's true that before you lost the leg there were other potential futures that included this leg, but at this moment, the one in which you no longer have two functioning legs, all of your potential futures from here on out no longer require this leg.

If you can let go of your attachment to those old stories and accept what is now fact (i.e., you have only one leg) rather than fight what is or compare your life to how it once was, you stand a much better chance of being able to move forward with your new life.

None of us know what our future holds. The meaning of what happens to us is all just stories, some empowering, others disempowering.

It's the disempowering stories that cause us emotional anguish, depression, tears, desperation and suffering.

That's why I say, whether you believe it's divine or just a better story, the belief that life happens *for* you, that every experience you have is serving you (although you may not yet know how) ultimately empowers you and brings much more peace to your life.

IT'S ALL JUST CHEMICALS ANYWAY

What is suffering, anyway? Yes, it's a story, but what do we feel from the story?

Emotions!

We often believe that we have no control over our emotions. In fact, we even project our emotions onto other people, claiming "they make me angry" or "they make me feel so loved".

Yet all of our emotions are only ever created inside of us, they are chemical reactions and electrical signals in our bodies.

When you feel angry, your amygdala, a region in the centre of your brain, releases a chemical signal. Epinephrine and norepinephrine combine with a low level of serotonin in the body, which prompts you to experience "anger."

Want to be a less angry person? Increase your serotonin levels.

It's not just anger either… Joy, fear, sadness — all the emotions you feel in response to the world around you and the stories you tell are simply chemicals reacting in your body.

When you admire a sunset, your brain is releasing oxytocin and dopamine, which triggers electrical impulses that race through the circuitry of your brain. When you feel attraction for someone, your brain is releasing dopamine, serotonin and norepinephrine, which triggers the physical attraction response in your body.

All these emotions are purely chemical. And if they are chemical reactions based on the stories we tell ourselves, then do you think it might be possible to create these feelings within ourselves at any time?

The answer is in my experience, yes!

I believe that deep down all any of us really want is to feel loved unconditionally and to feel like we are enough, just as we are.

Whether you are in pursuit of fame, fortune or spiritual enlightenment, it doesn't matter. At the base of it all, I would argue you are searching for unconditional love.

So what if I told you that you don't need to search for that love from anything external at all, that you can easily love yourself unconditionally and meet that need immediately?

You see nobody can make you feel loved. You do that to yourself. Someone does something that makes you generate the chemical reaction in your body that conveys the feeling of being loved.

When you say, "That person makes me feel so loved" you are simply projecting that feeling onto them. You could have that feeling without them, it's just that they've done something that has triggered it in you.

How do I know you can feel all emotions (including love) by yourself? Because I've done it.

When a long-term relationship of mine came to an end, I had the same stories that come with any break-up: "I'll never be loved again," "I'll spend my life alone," etc.

My coach said to me, "What do you think is missing from your life right now? What would you have if you were back with your partner that you don't have now?"

I replied, "Attraction, love, connection."

She said, "Okay, how do you do attraction?"

"How do I do attraction, what do you mean?" I responded.

"Well, you have a feeling, a sensation in your body that you call attraction, what does that feel like?" she replied.

And as I explained how I felt attraction for someone, all of a sudden that attraction was there in my body. I was sitting on the couch in my living room, completely alone. The only other presence near me was the voice on the end of the phone, and yet I was feeling the exact same sensations I would if I was in front of someone I was feeling deeply attracted to.

The same chemicals were being produced, the same electrical signals were being sent through my body and I was in a state of feeling attraction.

We then tried the same activity to generate the feelings of love and connection. Again, sitting all alone, I was able to produce the same feelings by triggering the right chemicals and physical reactions to produce the emotion in my body.

This proved to me that every feeling we seek in someone else we can find in ourselves. It's only because our stories tell us that they come from others that we assume it to be true.

The idea that someone else completes us is a fantasy. It seems romantic to think that, but this need for love and acceptance from others too often leads to co-dependency, which isn't healthy. Furthermore, if a relationship breaks down, this belief can generate tremendous suffering. I've heard of cases where people endured years of suffering after a break-up or divorce.

When I realised that I could feel any emotion I wanted whenever I wanted, I came to understand that there is never a reason for me to feel "incomplete" ever again.

You don't need completing, because you are already whole. You have everything you need in your mind and your body to produce all the emotions you could ever want.

Now I'm not saying it's not fun to link these emotions to others in our lives, especially emotions like love and joy. I'm also not saying that other human beings aren't great company, and that love and attraction aren't great things to feel around other people. What I am saying is you don't ever have to feel like you NEED someone else to feel fulfilled, happy and completely content with your life.

THE POINT OF A GOAL

Have you ever set yourself a goal and worked really hard and still not achieved it? How did you feel? Did you feel like a failure?

On the flip side, have you ever set a goal and absolutely smashed it? How did you feel then? You celebrated, right? Likely you felt unstoppable for 24-

48 hours and then, if you're like most people, you went back to focusing on the next goal. Am I right?

In my first book, *Red Means Go!*, I talked a lot about goal setting and outlined a process for breaking down your goals. You know what I missed? Emphasizing the value of celebration.

Even more than that, I missed the actual point of goals, and that's because, until recently, I didn't understand what that was. I now know that a goal isn't about achieving a specific outcome. In fact, attaching yourself to the story that this is the MUST-HAVE outcome can lead to suffering if you don't achieve it.

You have a comparison point to compare your life to. A thought that I was supposed to have done this by this date and I haven't.

Stories like…

I was going to have kids by 35.

I was going to be a millionaire by 30.

I was going to own a house.

I was going to be married and settled down.

My business is supposed to be profitable.

These are all great goals, but when you attach yourself to the outcome, you set yourself up for anxiety, stress and potential suffering.

Let me be clear that I'm not saying you shouldn't have goals?

No, this is not what I'm saying at all.

Absolutely, have your goal. Definitely, have your preferred outcome in mind and work towards that outcome.

Just do all that while being flexible and unattached to that specific outcome.

Let me explain...

In Red Means Go! I talked about the idea of being a sailing ship headed towards an island. You can be blown off course or end up in a completely different place, yet you can always course correct back to the island you first sought out to find.

I still agree with this; however, I'd like to add a new distinction: be open to the truth that the original island you were headed for may not be the best possible island for you.

As you go along in your journey and are blown off course and have mis-adventures, you may actually stumble across an even better island or someone else may tell you about a new island that just formed, and you can change your destination.

You don't need to be fixated on your original destination being your final outcome.

Why? Because this attachment to the outcome is what creates suffering in our lives. It's a comparison point.

When you realise that the true value of a goal isn't in the achievement of the outcome but in the growth of who you become in pursuit of it, everything changes.

It means that no matter what happens, you cannot fail when you set a goal. This takes the pressure off getting things "right." And besides, we've already discussed that "right" is just a label and a story we tell ourselves.

So instead of living in a halucinated future and missing today, enjoy the journey! Keep that future in mind but don't become overly attached to it, because there just might be something better on the horizon you don't know about yet.

If you set a goal and work for it but don't hit it, don't sweat it. I bet you became someone new, learned new skills, became more self-aware, shed old stories and created new ones and grew into a better version of yourself along the way.

As I've said before, the goal is never the real prize. The true prize is in the personal growth you experience in pursuit of your goals.

So set your intentions, get clear on your desired outcome, put your intention towards it and then detach from the outcome and see what happens.

THE SUMMARY

We've covered a lot in this chapter, so I want to boil it down for you into a simple recipe that you can follow and implement in your life.

I could have given you these steps along the way, but I didn't want to distract you from the context of each idea building upon the others. Now you have the context, so let's look at the steps:

- Step 1. Tell Yourself Better Stories
- Step 2. Examine Your Thoughts and Beliefs
- Step 3. Realise You Are Whole and Missing Nothing
- Step 4. Detach from Outcomes and Enjoy the Journey

Sounds simple right? That's because it is. Unfortunately, simple doesn't always mean easy.

In the next chapter, we'll look at ways you can integrate these concepts into your daily life.

4 STEPS TO BECOMING BULLETPROOF

- TELL YOURSELF BETTER STORIES
- EXAMINE YOUR THOUGHTS AND BELIEFS
- REALISE YOU ARE WHOLE AND MISSING NOTHING
- DETACH FROM OUTCOMES AND ENJOY THE JOURNEY

CHAPTER 5:
GOING INTO BATTLE
Living a Bulletproof Life

"The best way to make your dreams come true is to wake up." – Paul Valery

I'd like to help you put together an actionable plan to help you integrate the principles and strategies we've already covered into your daily life.

We're going to do that by creating a practice, something that you can do on a regular basis. Be that monthly, weekly or daily.

If the idea of a daily practice is foreign to you, I recommend that you start with a weekly practice to begin with and work your way up from there.

Why do we call it a practice? Because it's something that takes exactly that practice. It's not something you will ever say I'm done practicing now. Even as your skills and experience grow, you'll always find new ways to deeper the practice or new skills to practice.

To get in the habit of a new practice, it's important to do it at the same time every day/week/month. For example, my own daily practice begins as soon as I wake up and get out of bed.

Your practice will consist of two core components.

- Getting out of your head

- Reflecting on your journey

GETTING OUT OF YOUR HEAD

In chapter 2, I introduced the idea that you are not your mind. I also shared that I spent a large portion of my life living in my head. I want to give you some simple techniques you can use to get out of your head and into your body.

This is a practice that, if done daily (or even multiple times a day), will serve you in your pursuit of a bulletproof life.

Why get into your body? Because the more present and in your body you are, the easier it will be for you to catch when the mind is offering up hallucinations and stories that aren't serving you and the easier it will be for you to stay aligned to the four steps to becoming bulletproof.

So here's what, in my experience, best gets you out of your head and into your body:

- Exercise

I'm not talking about cardio exercises where it's easy to start drifting off in hallucination, I'm talking about pushing or pulling something heavy.

It doesn't matter if you do this in a gym or if you use your own bodyweight to work out at home. The key is to do something that requires intense focus and makes you feel your body.

It could even be a sport like boxing or Muay Thai. The point is to get you out of your head and into your body.

- Get Really Present

You might think, "I'm already present," but my bet is you aren't.

The best way to get present quickly is to focus on your five senses.

Stop the mind and focus on what you can hear right now in this moment. Can you hear a car going past? Can you hear an airplane overhead? Is your air conditioner or heater making a humming sound?

Now focus on what you can feel in this moment. Is there a breeze brushing past your cheeks? Can you feel the scratch of your jeans on your legs? What about the pressure of your butt touching the chair?

Now focus on what you can see. Don't search for things, see things! Look around you, what do you notice? Can you see scratches on the wall or tiny details you often miss? Can you make out the individual fibres in the carpet?

Is there anything you can smell? Maybe you can smell something floral, or the pollen in the air or the damp scent of rain.

What about your sense of taste? Can you taste what you last had to eat or drink? Is there anything else you can taste?

Focusing on these five senses brings your awareness back to your body and into the now. You're out of the hallucinations in your head and are truly present.

- Breathwork Meditation

I'm sure you've heard of meditation and maybe you've even heard of breathwork. Doing this on a daily basis has been a game-changing practice for me.

The act of breathing alone, when done in a particular way, can release stress, fire up the mind, increase mental clarity and, most importantly, get you into your body.

For your breathwork meditation, I recommend you start by using the track we have available for you at https://becomingbulletproofbook.com/resources and follow along with the guided meditation provided there.

If you know how to breathe (which you must if you're alive), then you can do breathwork meditation. It's literally as simple as breathing.

Reflecting on Your Life

The above strategies are meant to help get you back into your body. What's listed below will get you started with reflecting on your life.

- Gratitudes

Many studies have shown that the simple act of reflecting on what you're grateful for increases your mood and lowers stress. You may wish to write these in a journal, you may want to share them with your family over a meal or you may want to sit in silence and reflect on them by yourself. Find a practice that suits your lifestyle and gives you the biggest boost in feel-good chemicals.

How do you do it?

Think of something in your life — anything that you're really grateful for. Maybe it's something seemingly big, like a promotion at work, or the new contract you just won or the birth of your child. Maybe it's something seemingly small, like having a roof over your head, having access to hot water or the smile your partner gave you this morning.

There are no rules about what you can be grateful for. In fact, I'd say the more things you can truly feel grateful for while doing this process the better.

But don't pressure yourself to hit a certain number. Some days I can list out two whole pages of gratitudes, and other days only a handful of things come to mind.

Don't force it, feel it.

The other important thing to keep in mind when doing gratitudes is that it's not about creating a big list. It's actually about creating the chemicals inside your body, feeling the gratitude and basking in that feeling.

- Examine a Thought

In the previous chapter, I shared a process that I learned from Byron Katie, "4 Questions and a Turnaround," to examine a given thought, belief or situation.

Reflect for a moment and ask yourself, "How am I feeling?" If the feeling isn't one of complete peace, ask yourself, "What must I be believing to be true, for this to be in my experience?" The mind may then offer up a suggestion as to which thought, belief or story is creating your unsettled feeling.

This is the perfect opportunity to go through the 4 questions and examine the truth of this.

- Mirror Eye Gazing

This one may sound a little weird to you, but I swear it can change your life.

Start by finding a mirror and taking look at yourself to appreciate who you are.

Next, make direct eye contact with yourself. Look into your left eye (when looking into a mirror it's the eye on your left, when you're doing it with others their left is the eye on your right)

what do you notice about it? What colour is it? Can you see the small veins? What about the eyelids? Do you notice any little bumps or folds you can appreciate?

Now, while maintaining intense eye contact with yourself, say "I love you" over and over for at least 30 seconds.

Trust me. This is a powerful way to generate those chemicals that make you feel loved.

Really appreciate yourself in this moment, truly feel love for yourself. Once you're done, get on with your day.

Just Start

Add these practices to your daily, weekly and monthly routines and watch as your life transforms.

Don't try and do them all at once, especially from a standing start. Begin by adding one or two to your day or week, you can always come back and add more later once a routine has been established.

Go ahead and pick two of these that you can easily add into your routine for the next 2 weeks.

FINDING MOTIVATION

Here's the part you might find challenging...

Now that you realise that the world we live in is just a bunch of stories made up by people no smarter than you, what's the point of playing by the rules if you know the rules are all just made up anyway?

If you can generate the chemicals in your body to experience any emotion you want whenever you want, why get out of bed and do anything?

These are questions only you can answer. My role is to open the door and provide you with some tools to help you step through. You're the one who must ultimately choose how you walk through it.

Personally, my perspective is that it's like the characters in The Matrix. Even though they've escaped and are in the real world, they continually plug themselves back in. Then, once they're in the Matrix, they can play by some of its rules but choose to bend and even break others.

It all comes back to my favourite superhero, Superman. He has the power to rule the world and make everyone his slave, yet he chooses to be a hero who participates, contributes and adds value by serving others with his gifts.

Knowing what you know now gives you incredible power and gifts, like the ability to stay deeply present and not be caught up in your own hallucinations. The ability to tell yourself more empowering stories that serve you and those around you. The ability to lead yourself and others rather than blindly follow the crowd without question.

These gifts don't just benefit you; they benefit everyone you meet. So use them wisely.

Be the best version of you and be a guide for others to do the same. Shine a light in the darkness and lead by example, together we can all bring about a better world (or even a better universe) for everyone to enjoy.

4 WAYS TO BULLETPROOF YOUR LIFE

- GET OUT OF YOUR HEAD AND BACK INTO YOUR BODY
- FIND GRATITUDE ON A DAILY BASIS
- BREATHE DEEPLY
- EXAMINE A THOUGHT BEFORE YOU BELIEVE IT

OFFICIAL BONUS CONTENT

Get access to all the official bonus resources that support what's been discussed in this book, 100% Free...

VISIT

BecomingBulletproofBook.com/Resources

RECOMMENDED RESOURCES

BOOKS:

- *Red Means Go!* by Carl Taylor
- *Loving What Is* by Byron Katie
- *Sapiens* by Noah Yuval Harari

MOVIES:

- *The Matrix* (1999) directed by the Wachowski's
- *Behind The Curve* (2018) directed by Daniel J. Clark
- *Time* Interview with Neil DeGrasse Tyson (2008) https://www.youtube.com/watch?v=wiOwqDmacJo

WEBSITES:

- https://www.carltaylor.com

ABOUT THE AUTHOR

Carl Taylor is an entrepreneur, #1 Noteable business author, and Australia's leading freedom focused business strategist.

Carl lives his life striving to be a guiding light for others through his books, speaking, social media content and privately held businesses.

After more than 2 decades of walking the entrepreneurial journey of building and selling businesses, plus achieving financial freedom in his early 30's, life was looking pretty good for Carl.

Then one day in July 2019 his world came crashing down with the end of a 7 year relationship.

What came next was a journey of re-discovery, allowing Carl to truly embody and experience the incredible power of the human mind and come face-to-face with the stories we tell ourselves.

It was in his moments of greatest pain that he found his greatest strength.

You can learn more about Carl, his other books, and the work he does at carltaylor.com

Earlier Titles

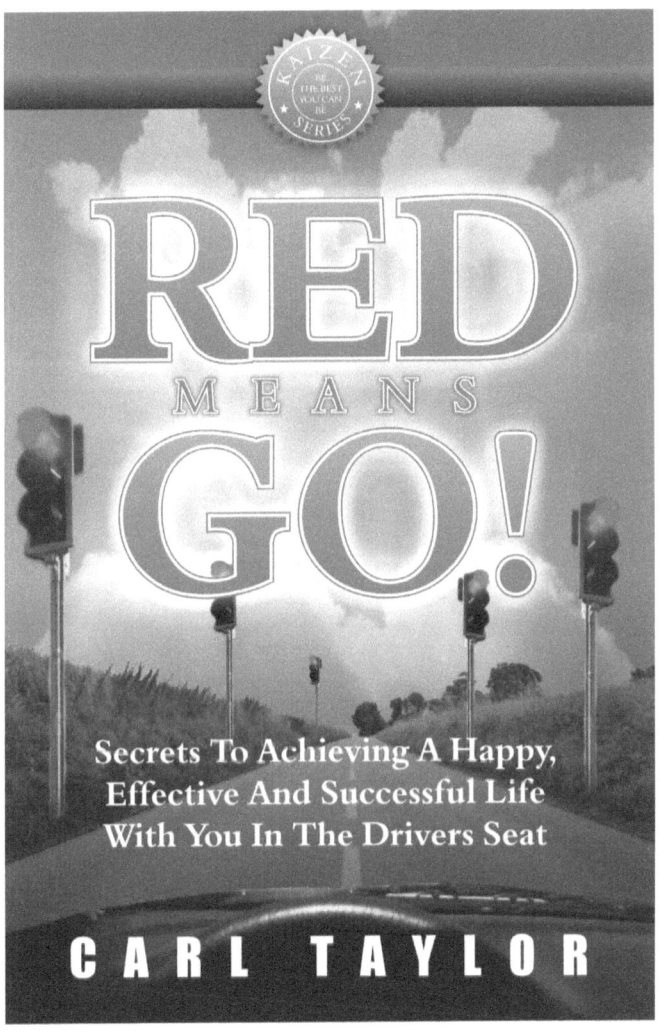

Available from RedMeansGoBook.com
or your favourite bookstore

INSIGHTS & ACTIONS

www.ingramcontent.com/pod-product-compliance
Lightning Source LLC
Chambersburg PA
CBHW030602020526
44112CB00048B/1179